Cezanne

Eleanor Marrack

MAGNA
BOOKS

Front Cover: *Village seen through Trees* (detail), 1890-1900 (Kunsthalle, Bremen)

Back Cover: *Still Life with Ginger Pot,* 1888-90 (Musée d'Orsay, Paris/Réunion des Musées Nationaux)

Published by Magna Books
Magna Road
Wigston
Leicester LE18 4ZH

Produced by Bison Books Ltd
Kimbolton House
117A Fulham Road
London SW3 6RL

ISBN 1-85422-480-8

Printed in Hong Kong

LIST OF PLATES

PAUL CEZANNE

1839-1906

The work of Paul Cézanne has had a vast, perhaps unparalleled, influence on twentieth-century art, and has been hailed variously as Impressionist, Post-Impressionist and, by Georges Braque, as the forerunner of Cubism. His long painting career spanned 50 years, a period which began with the first stirrings of Impressionism in the 1860s and ended only a year before Picasso painted his revolutionary *Les Demoiselles d'Avignon* in 1907. Cézanne participated in the first Impressionist exhibition in 1874 and is usually regarded as one of the foremost Impressionists, along with Monet, Pissarro, Renoir, Sisley, Degas and Morisot. From the late 1870s the group began to disperse and pursue individual interests, as the problem of reconciling a unified picture space with the Impressionists' determination to concentrate on the fleeting and casual became clearer.

Cézanne was less affected than his contemporaries by this apparent contradiction, as he was always more concerned than the others with closed and interlocking forms rather than with the passing effects of light. His colors and forms may be less naturalistic than those of, say, Monet, but they are also more balanced and structural; his works give a greater sense of solidity and permanence than the other Impressionists. It was this interest in the structural analysis of nature rather than in the representation of fugitive natural effects which animated the latter part of Cézanne's career. That this

was his conscious intention is suggested by his expressed desire to make of Impressionism 'something solid and enduring like the art of the museums.'

Cézanne was born in 1839 at Aix-en-Provence, son of a hat dealer who became a prosperous banker, owner of the town's only bank and one of the wealthiest men in the community. A powerful and domineering personality, Louis-Auguste Cézanne was deeply reluctant to accept his only son's choice of career. Although the financial security that the Cézanne family enjoyed enabled the young Cézanne to devote himself to painting from an early age, his father kept him on a meager allowance for many years and used the threat of stopping it altogether to keep his son in line.

From 1852 Cézanne attended the College Bourbon in Aix, where he became friendly with the future critic, journalist and novelist Emile Zola, a relationship that was to have a strong influence on the first half of his career. Zola moved to Paris in 1858 and survived a period of difficulty and poverty as a journalist before the success of his first major novel *Thérèse Raquin* in 1866. Cézanne stayed in Aix and was awarded second prize for drawing at the local Ecole des Beaux-Arts when he was 19. Uncertain of his direction, he enrolled in the local university to study law. When he decided that he wanted to be a painter, it took two years before Louis-Auguste could be persuaded to allow him to give up his studies and move to Paris, but finally, in April 1861, the

22-year-old Cézanne followed Zola to the artistic center of Europe.

Through his attendance at the informal life classes run by the Académie Suisse, Cézanne came into contact with some of the foremost avant-garde painters of the day, including Frédéric Bazille, Claude Monet, Auguste Renoir and Alfred Sisley. The radical work and theories of Gustave Courbet and Edouard Manet had challenged the official art world, as represented by the annual Salon; both artists had dared to hold exhibitions of their work outside the state-sponsored system. In 1863 Manet's *Le Déjeuner sur l'Herbe* caused a scandal, not only for its nudity in a contemporary setting, but also for Manet's bold technique, creating vivid contrasts of light and shade without the tonal gradations of standard academic practice.

The focus for avant-garde debate in the early 1860s was the Café Guerbois, where the writer and critic Edmond Duranty held court every Friday. Cézanne attended spasmodically, but was never at ease in the convivial surroundings and contributed little to the discussions. Always a solitary and rebarbative character, he was already revealing in his work that independence from contemporary theories and working practices that was to be one of his most fertile characteristics. Noted for his vehement attacks on official art, he nonetheless spent considerable periods copying in the Louvre, the state museum, and was much influenced by Rubens, Delacroix and the Baroque painters of the seventeenth century. Of his earliest life drawings, some are in the conventional academic manner of the day, while others demonstrate a fiercely independent, almost caricatural style.

Cézanne's earliest paintings are reworkings of old masters and ambitious nudes – indeed, his exploration of the traditional theme of the nude was to remain a recurring feature of his work. These abandon the idealized atmosphere and glossy surface paint of successful Salon pieces and are executed in a deliberately crude manner, in a rich, thick impasto laid on with a palette knife. Cézanne himself referred to the violent and impulsive effect as his 'couillarde' style, and paintings such as *The Murder* (1867-70) may be seen as the visual equivalent to the detailed, melodramatic realism of Zola's novels. Cézanne lacked the imitator's skill that in an earlier century would have been a prerequisite for a painting career; his early figures, such as *Bather and Rocks* (c.1864-68), are often grossly disproportionate in scale, as he firmly rejected facility in favor of power of expression.

From 1863-70 Cézanne spent a part of each year in the south of France, a pattern that he maintained throughout his life, and during this period his painting developed in a way that prepared him for the decisive years in the 1870s of working alongside Camille Pissarro. He began to experiment with still lifes, again a theme which was to recur throughout his working life, and for this change of subject matter adopted a more objective approach which recalls the work of Manet. The paint, although still thick, was applied more evenly, the forms were more fluid and linked more harmoniously together. Already Cézanne was revealing his unmistakable gift for building a picture and his subtle feeling for the interrelationships of color. The portrait of his father reading *L'Evénement*, a newspaper in which Zola had written a favorable review of his friend's work, is characteristic of this transitional style (*The Artist's Father*, 1866).

With the outbreak of the Franco-Prussian War in 1870, Cézanne moved south permanently for a couple of years. He took with him a young model, Hortense, but did not dare expose her to his family's censure and instead lived secretly with her in the village of l'Estaque, a small fishing port to the west of Marseilles. His fear of his father was such that, even when Hortense bore him a son, Paul, in 1872, he kept their existence secret; justifiably, as it turned out. When Louis-Auguste Cézanne did finally, six years later, discover the truth about his son's family, he instantly halved Cézanne's allowance. It was only in 1886, shortly before his father's death, that Cézanne, under pressure to legitimize his son, finally married Hortense.

In l'Estaque in 1870 Cézanne began to paint directly from nature but still, as in *Melting Snow at l'Estaque* (1870-71), with the dynamism and directness of expression that had characterized his earliest work. On his return to Paris in 1871 he came into close contact with Pissarro, a central figure in the Impressionist group and the only one to participate in all eight Impressionist exhibitions. Cézanne said in later life that Pissarro had been a father to him, and he certainly needed a sympathetic father figure to compensate for Louis-Auguste's irrational authoritarianism. In 1872 he moved to Pontoise, where Pissarro was working, and was taken under the older man's wing. This was Cézanne's first prolonged contact with a landscape painter and confirmed his belief in the practice of painting *en plein air*, rather than producing a polished version of a subject in the studio from sketches. Pissarro was also a man of intense and patient observation, and under his influence Cézanne finally abandoned his big dramatic brushstrokes in favor of smaller, supple dabs of paint that enabled him to cover the canvas with dense superimposed layers.

The association with Pissarro was a long and fruitful one, and marks the end of Cézanne's apprenticeship as a painter. In 1873 he moved his family to the village of Auvers on the Oise, a river much loved by avant-garde painters of the time, to be near to Pissarro. Together they set themselves to solve the problem created by the Impressionists' preoccupation with the evanescent effects of light: how to relate a mass of buildings to a surrounding landscape without destroying the unity of the image. Under Pissarro's influence Cézanne's palette became more luminous, his colors more vibrant and varied, and he virtually abandoned the dark earthy colors of his earlier work, as Van Gogh and Gauguin, also Pissarro's protegés, were later to do. *Landscape, Auvers* (1873) shows the still-young Cézanne at the start of his self-imposed task of renewing the European tradition of painting. With his obsessive dedication to what was before his eyes, he was in the process of developing an art that mediated between his perceptions of visible reality and the means by which he conveyed it – his painting.

Pissarro was instrumental in the decision of the group of avant-garde painters now meeting at the Café La Nouvelle-Athènes to hold an independent exhibition of paintings in 1874. This, sited in the recently vacated studio of the photographer Felix Nadar, became known as the first Impressionist exhibition, from a derogatory comment made about Monet's *Impression: Sunrise*. Despite some opposition from other members of the group, who found Cézanne moody and uncongenial, Pissarro ensured that his friend was included, and Cézanne showed *A Modern Olympia*, a tribute to and affectionate parody of Manet's scandalous *Olympia*, and two Pissarro-inspired landscapes.

He exhibited again with the Impressionists in 1877 but never wholly identified with the Impressionist group as such, or fully adopted their aims and techniques. Although he and Pissarro sometimes painted the same subject, like Monet and Renoir a few years earlier at La Grenouillère, there was never the same difficulty in identifying which work was by which artist. Cézanne's pictures of this period are less solidly constructed than much of his later work, but they are still more densely conceived and less airy and atmospheric than anything by Pissarro. The effect of Pissarro's influence was to open Cézanne's eyes to the possibility of achieving the structure and volume that he wanted through the use of color, as much as through force of expression.

In 1874, however, Cézanne's paintings attracted the most hostile of the almost totally negative criticism directed at the first Impressionist exhibition. The Irish writer George Moore's description of him as 'too rough, too savage a creature . . . his work may be described as the anarchy of painting' is typical of a reaction that was as much concerned with the artist's difficult character as with the singularity of his work. Through Renoir and the color merchant Père Tanguy, who both had a high opinion of Cézanne, however, he found a patron just when his fortunes seemed at their worst. Victor Chocquet was a former civil servant who had accumulated a substantial collection of works by Delacroix and younger avant-garde painters. He became a firm advocate of Cézanne's work and at his death owned some 35 canvases. The 16 paintings that Cézanne showed at the third Impressionist exhibition in 1877 were largely taken from Chocquet's collection.

Again, however, the critical response was almost wholly unfavorable, and Cézanne refused to participate in future Impressionist exhibitions. Although he continued to send works to the Salon from time to time, these were invariably unsuccessful. Denied exposure at either of the two available outlets, Cézanne was condemned to almost total obscurity. Only one critic, Georges Rivière, showed an understanding of Cézanne's purpose:

The paintings by Cezanne have the inexpressible charm of biblical and Greek antiquity. The movements of the figures are simple and grand like those in antique sculpture, the landscapes have an imposing majesty and his still lifes, so beautiful, so exact in their relationships of tones, have something of the solemnity of truth. In all his paintings the artist produces emotion, because he himself experiences before nature a violent emotion which his craftmanship transmits to the canvas.

In 1878 Cézanne returned to the south of France and rediscovered the landscape of his childhood with revelatory force. The climate in Provence was more stable than that of Normandy, the atmosphere clear, the light bright and constant; as Cézanne wrote to Pissarro, objects stood out 'like playing cards, red roofs against the sea.' Neither traditional art theory nor impressionist practice proved adequate to convey his reaction to the Provençal landscape, and he had to develop his own methods of 'organizing my sensations before nature.' The result can be seen in landscapes such as *Mountains at l'Estaque* (1886-90). The composition is clearly structured by means of a system of related arcs, which lead the eye into the depths of the picture space; colors are clear and bright and consciously ordered to give a sense of recession and distance; and individual but generalized elements interact with each other and with the picture space as a whole to create a balanced and harmonious image, which can be appreciated both as a landscape scene and as a rich pattern of color and texture.

From this time onward Cézanne worked almost wholly in isolation, spending most of his time in the south. He did not exhibit in Paris between 1877 and 1895 (apart from one unidentified painting at the Salon of 1882), and the only place where his paintings could be seen and bought was at Père Tanguy's shop. His sense of alienation was increased by the break-up of his long friendship with Zola after the publication of the latter's novel *L'Oeuvre* in 1886, which featured a fictional painter whom Cézanne took, probably rightly, to be himself. The unresolved status of Hortense and Paul continued to cause problems; in 1886, after a brief and restless sojourn in Paris, Cézanne installed them in the village of Gardanne while himself remaining at the Jas de Bouffan, the family home, and moved regularly between his two mutually hostile families. The situation was finally regularized in April 1886, when Cézanne and Hortense were married in the presence of Cézanne's parents. The family moved into the Jas de Bouffan and only six months later Cézanne *père* died, leaving the artist a substantial legacy. By this time the relationship with Hortense had become a distant one; after some months living with Cézanne's mother and sister, she and her son returned to Paris, apparently with Cézanne's full approval, and he resumed his habit of an annual visit to the Ile-de-France.

None of this prevented him from painting, however, and what has since been hailed as Cézanne's Post-Impressionist style was developed in almost total isolation from the contemporary art world. Like so many art historical terms, Post-Impressionism is in fact a posthumous identification, applied by the English art critic Roger Fry in 1910 to a varied exhibition of French painters, and specifically to Gauguin, Van Gogh and Cézanne himself. Historically, however, Cézanne, in his self-imposed quarantine, was not a part of Post-Impressionism. He described his position in 1889 in a letter to the Belgian Octave Maus:

I must tell you with regard to this matter (of exhibiting) that the many studies I made have given only negative results, and dreading the critics who are only too justified, I had resolved to work in silence until the day when I should feel myself able to defend in theory the results of my attempts.

The studies that Cézanne made in the 1880s of Gardanne, a hillside village of simple boxlike buildings, are characteristic of the radical implications of his work at this time. They have often been cited in connection with the development of Cubism and were among those of Cézanne's works that Braque and Picasso most admired.

Painting for Cézanne was always a slow and tortuous process. He worked laboriously, building up his paintings stroke by stroke, and a sudden change of weather could have him abandoning an image in despair. When the Provençal climate was unpropitious he would spend hours in his studio organizing and painting still lifes, to which he applied as much care and attention as to all his other work. Before this time, still life painting had been regarded as a fairly lowly genre. Courbet and Manet had both painted still lifes and these had been influential on the young Cézanne's efforts in this direction, but in the 1880s and 1890s he came back to the genre, bringing to it all the power and control he had acquired in the intervening period. In works such as *Still Life with Ginger Pot* (1888-90) and *Apples and Oranges* (1895-1900), his interest again lies in exploring the series of relationships between the objects he chooses and the complex structure that they create; he said that 'painting is not the servile copying of objects, but the discovery of harmony among numerous relationships.' With works such as these Cézanne raised the status of still life to the heights of artistic expression, and his achievements were continued in the twentieth century by Matisse, Braque and Picasso.

Another theme that recurred throughout Cézanne's artistic career was that of the nude figure in a landscape setting, a well-established tradition in the history of European painting and which links his work with that of masters such as Giorgione, Rubens and Watteau. In the final ten years of his life he worked on three large compositions of Bathers which are far removed from the open eroticism of some of his earlier nudes. These can be seen both as generalized references to Greek and Roman myth and as evidence of Cézanne's determination to sustain the notion of a Grand Tradition of painting by the use of traditional 'classical' subjects.

In 1895 the dealer Ambroise Vollard, at the suggestion of Pissarro, gave Cézanne a one-man show which served as his first public exposure for almost 20 years. Characteristically Cézanne did not attend the opening, but the result was to bring his work to the attention of younger artists and by the end of the century he was revered as a master by many of the avant-garde. In 1894 the painter and collector Gustave Caillebotte died and bequeathed his collection to the state, thus ensuring that by 1897 two of Cézanne's paintings were hanging in the Luxembourg. The growing critical appreciation of Cézanne's work was shrewdly exploited both by Vollard and by the artist's son Paul, who seems to have inherited his grandfather's business sense. Cézanne himself was careless about the fate of his work, and would leave paintings in fields or hotel rooms, or give them away. He was more moved by Maurice Denis' painting *Hommage à Cézanne*, shown at the Salon des Indépendants in 1901, which depicted a Cézanne still life being admired by a group of painters including Bonnard, Vuillard and Denis himself in Vollard's shop; the painting was bought by the novelist André Gide.

As Cézanne grew older and more infirm, his visits to Paris became less frequent and his commitment to the landscape of his youth came increasingly to dominate his work. Between 1895 and his death he produced a series of paintings of the Mont Sainte-Victoire, five miles east of Aix. The rich variety of these (*Mont Sainte-Victoire*, 1904-06), from closely-organized analytical studies to loose veils of color which float on a half-empty canvas, demonstrate the continuing vitality of his absorbed interaction with the natural world. He wrote to his son shortly before his death:

I must tell you that, as a painter, I am becoming more clear-sighted before nature, but that with me the realization of my sensations is always painful. I cannot attain the intensity that is unfolded before my senses . . . Here on the bank of the river, the motifs multiply, the same subject seen from different angles gives a subject for study of the most powerful interest and so varied that I think I could occupy myself for months without changing place, simply bending a little more to the right or left.

In 1899 the Jas de Bouffan was sold and Cézanne moved into an apartment in the center of Aix. A couple of years later he acquired a piece of land just outside the town where he had a studio constructed, and it became his habit to walk there each day. He was working on a portrait of his gardener Vallier when he collapsed and died on 22 October 1906.

Cézanne's reputation continued to develop rapidly in the early twentieth century. In 1904 the salon d'Automne gave him a special exhibition, and in 1907 Vollard organized a major retrospective of his work. By 1914 his position as a key figure was sufficiently well-established for the English critic Clive Bell to hail him as 'the Christopher Columbus of a new continent of form'.

THE VILLAGE OF GARDANNE
Oil on canvas
36¼×29⅜ inches (92×74.6 cm)
Brooklyn Museum, New York

Above
BATHER AND ROCKS, *c.*1860-66
Oil on canvas transferred from plaster
66×41½ inches (167.6×101.7 cm)
Chrysler Museum, Norfolk, Virginia
Gift of Walter P Chrysler Jr

Right
THE ARTIST'S FATHER, 1866
Oil on canvas
78⅛×47 inches (198.5×119.3 cm)
National Gallery of Art, Washington

10

THE MURDER, 1867-70
Oil on canvas
25¼×31¾ inches (64×81 cm)
Walker Art Gallery, Liverpool

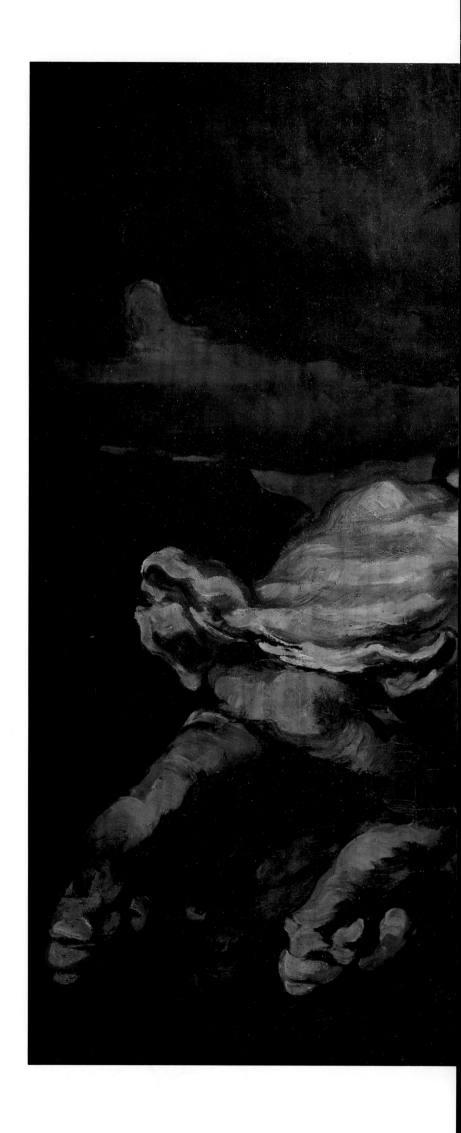

MELTING SNOW AT L'ESTAQUE, 1870-1
Oil on canvas
28¾×36¼ inches (73×92 cm)
Private collection, Switzerland

THE SEINE AT BERCY, 1873-5
Oil on canvas
23⅝×29½ inches (60×75cm)
Kunsthalle, Hamburg

LANDSCAPE, AUVERS, *c.*1873
Oil on canvas
18¼×21¾ inches (47.4×55.7 cm)
Philadelphia Museum of Art

Above
SELF-PORTRAIT, 1873-6
Oil on canvas
25¼×20½ inches (64×52 cm)
Musée d'Orsay, Paris

Right
MADAME CÉZANNE IN A RED ARMCHAIR, *c.*1877
Oil on canvas
28½×22 inches (72.5×56 cm)
Museum of Fine Arts, Boston

VILLAGE SEEN THROUGH TREES, 1890-1900
Oil on canvas
25½×31⅞ inches (65×81 cm)
Kunsthalle, Bremen

THE CARD PLAYERS, *c.*1892
Oil on canvas
25½×32⅜ inches (65×82 cm)
Metropolitan Museum of Art, New York

APPLES AND ORANGES, 1895-1900
Oil on canvas
28¾×36¼ inches (73×92 cm)
Musée d'Orsay, Paris

An Old Woman with a Rosary, *c.*1896
Oil on canvas
31⅞×24 inches (81×61 cm)
National Gallery, London

IN THE PARK OF THE CHÂTEAU NOIR, *c.*1898
Oil on canvas
36¼×28¾ inches (92×73 cm)
Musée de l'Orangerie, Paris

Above
THE BATHERS, 1899-1904
Oil on canvas
20¼×24¼ inches (51.3×61.7 cm)
Chicago Art Institute

Right
ROCKS AND BRANCHES AT BIBÉMUS, 1900-4
Oil on canvas
24×19¾ inches (61×50 cm)
Petit Palais, Paris

40

MONT SAINTE-VICTOIRE, 1904-6
Oil on canvas
23⅝×27½ inches (60×70 cm)
Öffentliche Kunstsammlung
Kupferstichkabinett, Basle

42

ACKNOWLEDGMENTS

The publisher wishes to thank Martin Bristow, who designed this book, and the following agencies and institutions, who supplied illustrative material.

Courtesy of the Art Institute of Chicago: page 40 (The Amy McCormick Memorial Collection, 1942.457)

The Brooklyn Museum, New York: page 9 (Ella C Woodward and Augustus T White Memorial Funds, 23.105)

The Chrysler Museum, Norfolk, Virginia: page 10 (Gift of Walter P Chrysler Jr)

Kunsthalle Bremen: pages 32-33

Kunsthalle Hamburg: pages 16-17

The Metropolitan Museum of Art, New York: pages 34-35 (Bequest of Stephen C Clark, 1960)

Musée de l'Orangerie, Paris/photos courtesy RMN: pages 26, 39 (Collection Jean Walters and Paul Guillaume)

Musée d'Orsay, Paris/photos courtesy RMN: pages 20, 30, 36-37

Collection of the Museum of Fine Arts, Boston: pages 21 (Bequest of Robert Treat Paine 11), 22-23 (Bequest of John T Spaulding)

National Gallery of Art, Washington: page 11 (Collection of Mr and Mrs Paul Mellon)

National Gallery, London: page 38

National Museums and Galleries on Merseyside: The Walker Art Gallery, Liverpool: pages 12-13

National Museum of Wales: pages 28-29

Offentliche Kunstsammlung Basel, Kunstmuseum/ photo Colorphoto Hans Hinz: pages 42-43

Petit Palais, Paris/photos Musées de la Ville de Paris © SPADEM 1990: pages 24-25, 41

Philadelphia Museum of Art: pages 18-19 (Samuel S White 111 and Vera White Collection)

Private Collection, Switzerland/photo H Humm: pages 14-15

Pushkin Museum, Moscow/photo SCALA: pages 27, 31